MISTER MAGNIFICENT'S MAGICAL MERRIMACK ADVENTURE!

INGRID HESS

Mister Magnificent's Magical Merrimack Adventure!

Copyright © 2016 by Ingrid Hess

This book was created in partnership with the University of Massachusetts Lowell, the Tsongas Industrial History Center and Lowell National Historical Park. All rights reserved. No part of this book may be reproduced in any manner whatsoever without written permission except in the case of brief quotations embodied in critical articles and reviews. Printed in the United States of America. Published by Ingrid Hess.

Created by Ingrid Hess; Edited by Sheila Kirschbaum and Linda Sopheap Sou.

ISBN-978-0-692-71484-3

Library of Congress Control Number: 2016908084

To request information please visit the following websites:
www.nps.gov/lowe
www.uml.edu/tsongas

Special thanks!

Creating a great children's book takes a village. We are grateful to the following people for their help: Celeste Bernardo, Luis Falcón and the College of Fine Arts, Humanities & Social Sciences at UMass Lowell, Pat Fontaine, Sheli Turocy, MaryBeth Clark, Becky Warren, Kristin L. Gallas, Dave Byers, Sue Andrews, Tess Shatzer, Anita Greenwood, JehanneMarie Gavarini, Christoph Strobel and Valerie Daneau's third graders at Bartlett Elementary School in Lowell.

"Is it time to go yet?" asked Socheata for the third time that afternoon.

Socheata's parents bustled around the kitchen cooking. They were making food for the Water Festival. Socheata attended the festival every year and loved it.

"Listen, honey, it won't be time to go for two more hours," said her mother. "You can either help me finish these treats, or you can go outside and find something interesting to do. Just make sure that you get to the festival in time for supper."

Socheata hurried outside. She saw her friends Clarice, Nicholas, and Patrick under the oak tree peering at a piece of paper.

"Hey, what are you looking at?"

"Something incredible," said Nicholas, adjusting his glasses.

"This paper says there's a free hot air balloon ride to the festival," said Clarice.

"Mom said I should find something interesting to do," said Socheata. "This sounds perfect."

"Awesome," said Patrick.

The four kids sat down and thought happy thoughts about hot air balloons. Soon Nicholas stood up.

"Hey, I see something. Look up there!"

Sure enough, down from the sky floated the most incredible hot air balloon the children had ever seen. Inside was a very old-fashioned looking man.

"Are you Mr. Magnificent?" asked Socheata.

"At your service," said the man. "I hear you need a ride to the Water Festival. Hop aboard. We mustn't be late."

The children climbed aboard.

"Are you sure it's safe?" asked Socheata.

"What if we fall out?" asked Nicholas.

"Will this balloon pop?" asked Clarice.

"Not to worry, not to worry," said Mr. Magnificent.
"I'll get you there lickety-split and all in one piece."

"Awesome," said Patrick, and up they floated
 towards the clouds.

Once they were high in the air, Socheata spoke up.

"What makes this hot air balloon tour magical?"

"Great question," said Mr. Magnificent. "In this balloon, when you look over the edge, you don't just see down to the ground, you also see back in time."

"Awesome," said Patrick.

"That's impossible," said Nicholas.

"Try it," said Mr. Magnificent.

Nicholas peeked over the edge. Instead of seeing his neighborhood, he saw forests and fields where women and children were farming. A few men were hunting and fishing.

"Who are they?" asked Nicholas.

"They're the first people who lived on this land," said Mr. Magnificent. "Native Americans lived in New England for many generations. The Merrimack River was extremely important, because it was the home of so much wildlife, and its shores were good farmland. The river provided great places to farm, hunt, and fish."

"Who wants to look next?" asked Nicholas.

Native Americans

The Native American communities who lived near the Merrimack River for a very long time were part of the Penacook group. Important rulers of the Penacook included Passaconaway and Wannalancit. These names are used for places in New England today.

The Merrimack River and the Pawtucket Falls were important to the Native American way of life. The river provided food and transportation. During the spring, Native Americans came to the falls to plant corn, beans, and squash. They also gathered salmon and other fish from the river.

European settlers did not recognize Native American ownership of the land. In the 1600s, the Europeans pushed out most of the local groups. Many of these Native Americans fled north. Some descendants of these early Americans still hold pow-wows and other ceremonies that keep their culture alive.

FASCINATING FACT
Corn was as important for Eastern Native Americans as buffalo were to Western Native Americans.

Clarice jumped up and looked over the side of the basket.

"From this high up, the farms look like a giant quilt," she said.

Mr. Magnificent continued his story.

"When the European settlers first arrived, they used the Merrimack River valley for farmland. Like the Native Americans, they knew the soil along the banks of the river would be ideal for growing crops. Unfortunately, the colonists wanted the land for themselves, and they forced the local tribes to move away."

"That's not very fair," said Clarice. "The Native Americans were here first."

"You're right," said Mr. Magnificent. "Over the past 200 years, many changes have happened on the shores of the Merrimack River. Some of these changes haven't been fair."

Colonial Settlement

When Europeans first came to New England, most lived on farms. Families worked hard to make what they needed for daily life. They bartered (traded) for things they couldn't make themselves. One of the most time-consuming chores for colonial settlers was making cloth. Wool needed to be cleaned, straightened, and spun into yarn before weaving could begin. This weaving was typically done on hand looms.

Colonists also lived in towns and cities. Many became skilled craftspeople. Several trades were common:

- blacksmithing
- tailoring
- shoemaking

Craftspeople often worked in small workshops and owned their own tools.

Colonial Americans used the Merrimack River to travel and transport goods, but the Pawtucket Falls made river travel difficult. The full potential of the Merrimack River had yet to be discovered.

FASCINATING FACT
Before 1800, bartering for goods was far more common than selling items for cash.

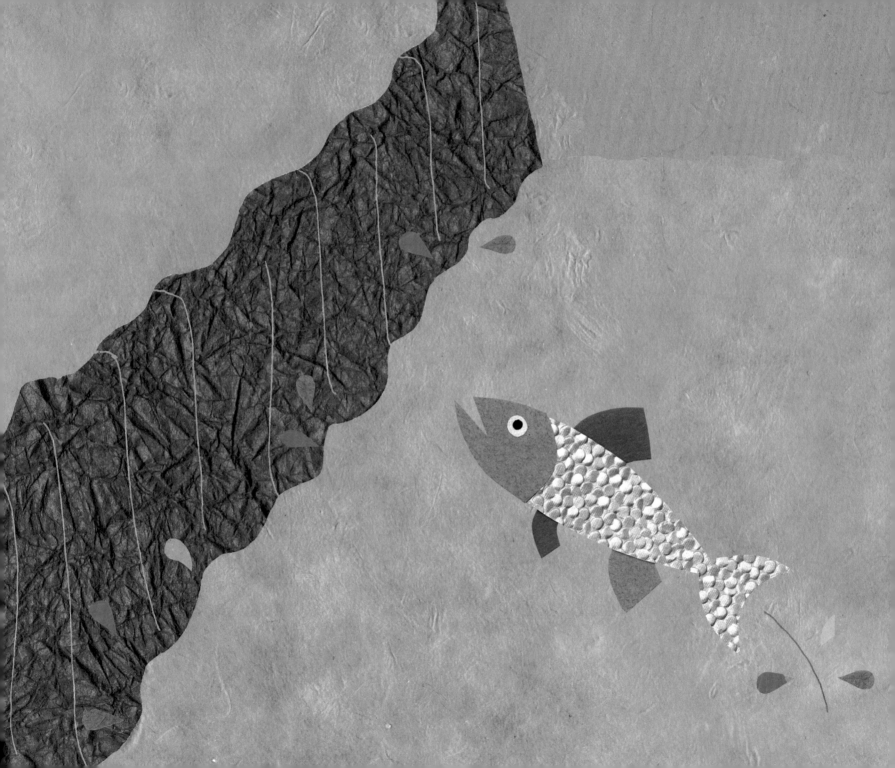

"It's my turn," said Socheata. She peeked over the edge. "Wow! I see a waterfall!"

"Awesome," said Patrick.

"In fact," said Mr. Magnificent, "the waterfall really *is* awesome. It's the entire reason your city of Lowell is here."

"What do you mean?" asked Socheata.

"Waterfalls create a lot of power," said Mr. Magnificent. "Because of the waterfall, people built mills. The water turned the waterwheels that powered the machines in the mills."

"How did they get the water from the river to the waterwheels?" asked Nicholas.

"They dug a very impressive canal system," said Mr. Magnificent, "one of the best in the world. Because of this canal system, the mills in this region were quite successful."

"Did they build a lot of mills?" asked Clarice.

"Take a look," said Mr. Magnificent.

The Canal System

In 1814 a man named Francis Cabot Lowell wanted to build a large textile mill. Because there was no electricity, Lowell had to build the mill where there was a natural power source. He built his mill in Waltham, Massachusetts, and used water power. The mill was a success.

Mr. Lowell's business partners knew of a nearby area on the Merrimack River that was perfect for building more mills. The river fell 32 feet over about one mile. They decided to build a system of canals that took water from the high level, channeled it through the mills, and then returned it to the river at a lower level. These businessmen hired mostly Irish immigrants from Boston to dig the canals. By 1850 the canal system was almost 6 miles long and powered 10 major mill complexes.

The mill owners thought of the river as their property, as something that could be controlled for their own profit. One thing is certain . . . without the waterfall and the canals, there would have been no large textile mills in Lowell.

FASCINATING FACT
Five hundred men with shovels worked for 17 months to dig the first 1½ miles of the canal system.

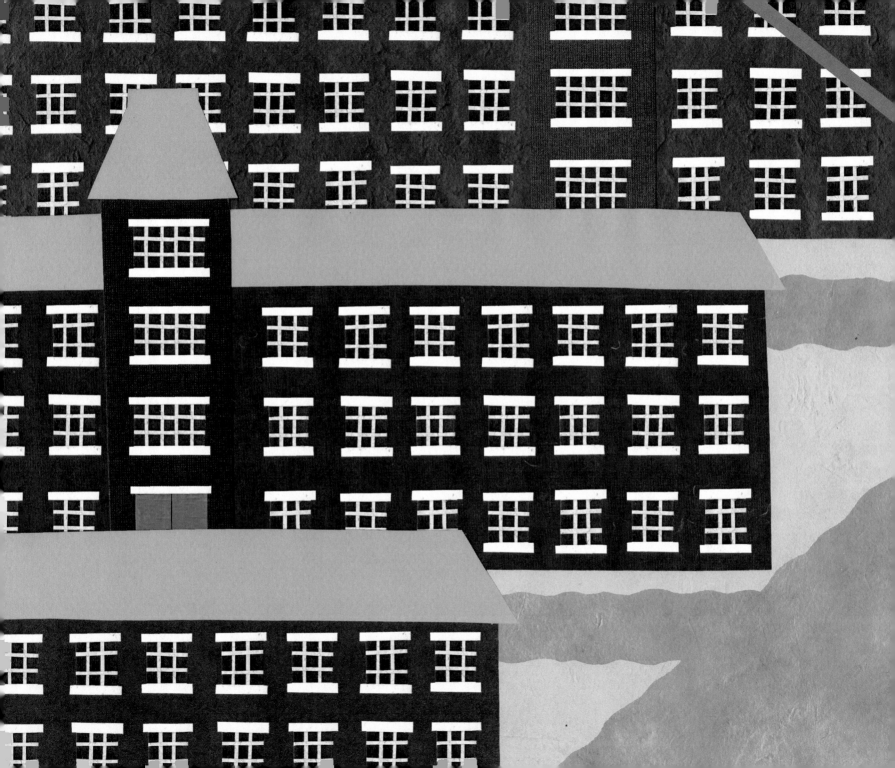

The four kids peeked over the side. Mill buildings were everywhere.

"What did they make inside the mills?" asked Nicholas.

"Another great question," said Mr. Magnificent. "The mills were built to make cloth—millions and millions of yards of cloth. Of course, people made cloth before these mills were built. But here in Lowell, an entire city of mills was planned and built to manufacture cloth. It was the first city like it in the country, and it was a huge success."

The Mills

In 1810 Francis Cabot Lowell traveled to Great Britain to learn about how British mills operated. The English power loom wove cloth much faster than hand weavers could. English mill owners did not want other countries to have this invention, so the British government prohibited anyone from sending a power loom to another country. Mr. Lowell visited factories that used power looms. He memorized how the looms worked.

When Lowell returned home in 1812, he and a mechanic named Paul Moody built the first power loom in the United States. With this new technology, Lowell was able to build a water-powered factory in which all the steps of making cloth took place under one roof.

After Lowell's death in 1817, some of Lowell's partners built other mills that used water from the Merrimack River for power. The first mill opened in 1823, and by 1848 ten major manufacturing corporations employed 12,000 workers. The city that was formed was named Lowell. By 1850, Lowell had grown to more than 30,000 inhabitants.

FASCINATING FACT
The Lowell mills were so successful that they were copied. Factory cities sprang up all over New England.

"Who worked in the mills?" asked Clarice.

Mr. Magnificent reached into his pocket and pulled out a pair of binoculars.

"Here," he said, handing them to Clarice. "Take a closer look."

Clarice looked through the binoculars. She saw many women and a few men lining up for work.

"Those are the mill girls," said Mr. Magnificent, "local young women who left their families' farms and moved to the city to work in the mills."

The "Mill Girls"

Lowell mill managers hired young, single women, mostly ages 14 to 25, from farms across New England. The bosses hired these Yankee women for many reasons:

- Women already knew how to make cloth.
- The bosses believed women would accept lower wages than men would.
- Women had few other opportunities for paid work.

Yankee women took the jobs for many reasons:

- The pay was higher than women could find in other jobs.
- Their earnings helped support their families.
- The city offered social, cultural, and religious opportunities, including lectures, exhibitions, and plays.

The "mill girls" lived in boardinghouses that the mill owners had built. Usually 30 to 40 women lived together in each boardinghouse. They were expected to attend church regularly and behave properly. The boardinghouses provided a supportive environment for the workers. Some workers stayed for many years.

FASCINATING FACT
Nearly 10,000 Yankee women left New England towns to work in Lowell.

"I see a few young children, too." said Clarice.

"Children were a big help in the mills," said Mr. Magnificent. "Young girls helped in the spinning room. Young boys ran along the canals carrying messages between the engineers, the mill bosses, and the gatehouse keepers. In fact, when I was a wee lad, I was a runner boy."

"That's impossible," said Socheata. "If you were a runner boy, you would now be over 150 years old."

"Didn't I mention earlier that this hot air balloon tour is magical?" asked Mr. Magnificent, and he winked.

"Awesome," said Patrick.

Girls and Boys

By the mid-1800s, the textile mills in Lowell produced more than one million yards of cloth each week. In addition to hiring adult workers, mill owners occasionally hired children. The mill owners hired young girls, ages 9 to 13, to be bobbin girls. Their job was to remove the bobbins filled with yarn from the spinning frames and replace them with empty ones.

Gatehouse keepers controlled the level of water in the canals, which affected the speed of the machines. Because the telephone had not yet been invented, the mill bosses had to figure out a way to send messages to the gate tenders when the water level needed adjusting. What they did was hire young boys to be runner boys. These boys ran along the canals delivering messages.

While girls and boys in the mills worked hard, the work wasn't constant. Bobbin girls worked about 15 minutes out of every hour. In 1836, Massachusetts passed its first child labor law requiring children under 15 working in factories to attend at least three months of school per year.

FASCINATING FACT
By 1848 Lowell's mills produced 50,000 miles of cotton cloth each year, enough to circle the earth twice.

The balloon floated along peacefully until—

"Duck!" screeched Mr. Magnificent.

Socheata, Clarice, Nicholas, and Patrick screamed. They immediately crouched down and covered their heads. Mr. Magnificent burst out laughing.

"No, no, no," he said. "I didn't mean you were supposed to get down. I meant, 'Here comes my good friend, Duck.'"

Into the hot air balloon flew a duck. The duck perched on Mr. Magnificent's shoulder and quacked a friendly hello.

"Why is there a duck all the way up here?" asked Nicholas.

"If you take a peek over the edge, I think you'll understand," said Mr. Magnificent.

Nicholas stuck his head over the edge.

"Something stinks!" he said.

"You're right." said Mr. Magnificent. "Unfortunately, the mills created a lot of pollution. Waste from the mills spilled into the river. That pollution caused major problems. The salmon that used to be so plentiful started to die. People who depended on the Merrimack River for drinking water became sick. Duck always comes and visits me during this part of the tour. He'd rather avoid all that stench."

Working Conditions

Working in the mills could be unpleasant—in fact, it could be dangerous! Here are some of the poor conditions workers had to endure.

- **Noise**
  The machines were very noisy. Many workers lost their hearing.

- **Poor ventilation**
  The factories had poor ventilation. The humid, dusty air of the mill made many workers ill.

- **Dangerous machines**
  The moving parts of the looms weren't covered, so accidents were common.

- **Speed-ups and stretch-outs**
  Owners increased both the speed and the number of looms that workers operated.

- **Poor drinking water**
  People dumped dyes, chemicals, and human waste into the river. Drinking the polluted water sometimes made people sick.

FASCINATING FACT
The "mill girls" worked 6 days a week, for up to 14 hours a day— sometimes standing the entire time!

Socheata looked over the side.

"Oh, no," she said. "I think there's trouble brewing down below."

"Great observation," said Mr. Magnificent. "The mill girls are protesting."

"What are they protesting?" asked Nicholas.

"Pollution wasn't the only problem the mill girls had to deal with," said Mr. Magnificent. "Working conditions weren't all that grand. Low wages, long working hours, and loud machines were everyday occurrences. Many mill girls walked out."

"Did their protests work?" asked Socheata.

"While they didn't get everything they wanted right away, over time their efforts made a big difference," said Mr. Magnificent.

Protesting

The first strikes by textile factory workers in U.S. history took place in Lowell. "Mill girls" led these strikes. The strikers had several complaints:

- long work days and pay cuts
- increased speed of machines
- increased number of machines for each worker

Mill owners were very powerful and could fire troublemakers. They thought it was unacceptable for women to complain. It took courage for the "mill girls" to protest these conditions. One brave protester was a 10-year-old girl who led an entire floor of workers out in protest. Unfortunately, their protests were mostly ignored. These strikes failed for a number of reasons:

- Mill owners worked together to prevent any mills from giving in to workers' demands.
- New immigrants were willing to take the jobs.

Even though not every strike succeeded, the "mill girls" didn't give up. Their protests resulted in a law in 1874 that made a 10-hour work day the legal limit for women and children in Massachusetts.

FASCINATING FACT
During the 1830s, the "mill girls" earned between $12 and $14 a month.

Socheata, Clarice, Nicholas and Patrick took turns looking through the binoculars. Each child saw a different group of people.

"Why are there so many kinds of people down there?" asked Socheata.

"Very good, very good," said Mr. Magnificent. He was clearly delighted. "Yet another great observation. Did you know that the United States is made up of many groups of immigrants?"

"Yes," said Socheata. "That's because people from all over the world have moved here to start a new life."

"That's right," said Mr. Magnificent. "And the Merrimack River valley is a great example of this immigration. Over the years, many different groups of people have moved away from their homelands to start a new life here."

"My Greek ancestors immigrated here," said Nicholas.

"So did my ancestors," said Socheata. "We're from Cambodia."

"My family did, too" said Clarice. "We just immigrated from Kenya, and I know Patrick's ancestors came from Ireland."

"Awesome," said Patrick.

Immigrants

For 30 years, Yankee women filled most of the jobs in the mills. In the middle of the 1800s, changes started to occur. Irish immigrants moved to Lowell because of a famine in Ireland. These new residents were willing to work for less pay. They gradually joined Yankee women in the mills.

French-Canadian immigrants moved to Lowell in the 1860s and 70s. By the end of the 1800s, immigrants from Greece, Poland, Portugal, and other countries started to arrive. With all the available workers, wages became even lower. Whole families had to work in the mills to make enough money to survive.

In the late 20th century, immigrants continued to come to Lowell. Many people arrived from Southeast Asia, Latin America, and other parts of the world. In the early 21st century, refugees from the Middle East and Africa settled in Lowell.

FASCINATING FACT
In 1900, more than 40% of Lowell's residents were born in another country.

The balloon continued to float closer and closer to the Water Festival.

"Are we there yet?' asked Nicholas.

"We've almost arrived," said Mr. Magnificent. "Take one last peek over the edge, and you can see what a great place the Merrimack River valley is today."

Socheata, Clarice, Nicholas, and Patrick looked over the edge one last time.

Mr. Magnificent pointed down. "You see, the Merrimack River and its remarkable canal system still exist today. In fact, they are part of a National Park. The city surrounding the river and the canals is made up of a rich blend of people from many different countries. You really are extremely lucky to live in a place with such a great history, such an interesting combination of cultures, and such a bright future."

"Awesome," said Patrick.

ຄືຄືບຸດຄູກຮູ້ຮູກ   ບຸນຊ່ວງເຮືອ
ງານແຂ່ງເຮືອສາຍສັມພັນธ์ประจำปีที่
SOUTHEAST ASIAN WATER FESTIVAL

Lowell Today

In 1972, the U.S. Congress passed the Clean Water Act. As a result, Lowell and other cities, along with local citizen groups, cleaned up the Merrimack River. Because of their efforts, the water in the river and the canal system is now healthy. These improvements help the region in many ways:

• Water provides hydroelectric power.
• Water provides recreation opportunities, such as fishing, boating, and swimming.
• Clean drinking water is available.

The city of Lowell is also thriving. Organizations like the University of Massachusetts Lowell, the Tsongas Industrial History Center, and Lowell National Historical Park are working together to make Lowell a great place to live and learn.

Finally, Lowell continues to grow stronger through a rich blending of cultures. Descendants of the original Native Americans and all the immigrants groups who followed play an important role in shaping this city. Lowell is a truly remarkable place with a rich history, an exciting present, and a bright future.

FASCINATING FACT
Lowell is known as the "Mill City" or the "Spindle City."

The hot air balloon started to descend. When it arrived safely on the ground, the four children climbed out.

"Wow, Mr. Magnificent, thanks so much!" said Socheata. The other children nodded their agreement.

"Glad to be of service," said Mr. Magnificent. "Enjoy the festival, and be in touch if you ever find yourselves in need of another tour." With that, Mr. Magnificent and Duck floated back up into the air in search of their next adventure.

Socheata saw her mom coming across the field.

"Hi, honey. I'm so pleased you and your friends made it here on time. Did you manage to find something interesting to do?"

"We sure did," said Socheata.

"Here, have some food," said Socheata's mother. "I saved the best treats for you and your friends."

"Thanks," said Nicholas.

"These are delicious," said Clarice.

"What do you think, Patrick?" asked Socheata.

"Awesome!" said Patrick.